A

Teenager's

Guide

to the

Workplace

Karen S. Hinds

New Books Publishing
Boston, Massachusetts

New Books Publishing
Boston, Massachusetts

Hinds, Karen S.
A Teenager's Guide to the Workplace

ISBN 0-9679861-1-7

Library of Congress Control
Number: 2001117779

Cover Design: Culpdesign
culpdesign@mediaone.net

Cover Photograph: Sandy Middlebrooks

Hair: Jonathan's for Hair, Boston

ACKNOWLEDGMENTS

Thank you to the following people who helped make this book a reality. **To** the students of Charlestown High School: Dozie Azotam, Thomas Carroll, Rashid Al-Kaleen, Rodney Araujo, Fernando Corporan, Orlando Rivera, Edward Samedy, Kerlyne Laguerre, Thy Le Tran, Kimaada Haygood, Janel Aubry, Golita Bazile, Edicaira Moreta, Tom Thin, Nakia Dean; **To** Kathleen Hassan and her vibrant Milton Girls group; **To** Michelle Foley, Kara K. Chisholm, Cara Hebard, Krista Morrison, Amanda Hebard, Alicia Anne Driscoll, Amelia Sloane, Kristy Needham, Lauren "Lai" Faith, Christina Goss, Josh Bruno, Warren Toland, Teresa Feeney, Raphael Edwards and John Sadler of East Boston High; and **To** all the adults who truly believe and act upon their convictions that our youth are the future of tomorrow; your hard work is making a difference.

TABLE OF CONTENTS

CHAPTER 9: MONEY MATTERS

CHAPTER 10: LOOKING OUT
FOR NUMBER ONE

CHAPTER 11: EXTRAS TO KNOW

CONCLUSION: VALUING DIFFERENCES

APPENDIX
About the Author
Order Form

PREFACE

You're probably reading this book because a teacher, parent, or the company you work for bought it for you. Some of you may have gotten it on your own. If you're in the former category you're probably wondering, "What is it with all this work stuff? How hard could it be to show up, do what they say, and get paid?"

For some people it is not hard at all. However, there are rules in the workplace that no one talks about. There are norms or unspoken rules that you are expected to live by when you go into the workplace. It does not matter if you are a bagger at a grocery store, a cashier at a fast food restaurant, or a mail clerk in an office building downtown, the rules still apply.

You may ask, "How am I supposed to know these rules if they are unspoken?" This book will help you understand the unspoken rules of the work world and create a foundation for excellent work habits, success, and achievement in your future career.

CHAPTER ONE

TIME TO GO TO WORK

. I Need a Job Now

. Ten Ways to Find a Job

I NEED A JOB NOW

You've probably been thinking about getting a job for a while. You may feel the need to earn some money of your own, maybe you want to show your parents that you can be responsible, or you want to buy a car, and some of you may need to work to help with family responsibilities or save for college. Whatever your reason, you feel it's time to bring in a paycheck.

The first thing you should know is that there are many different kinds of jobs for teenagers. Almost all companies, at some point in the year, hire teenagers, so you may have many choices.

The second thing you should consider is the field you want to work in. Do you like fashion and working with people? Then the retail industry might be best suited for you. Are you shy and prefer talking on the phone? Then consider a job where you can be an office assistant. There are still more industries to consider: food, hotel and tourism, computer, and the list goes on. Try to find a job in a field you may like or be adventurous and try a new industry.

The third thing you should take to heart is that nowadays, employees must think of their employer as their primary customer. That is the way to advance your own career.

Whether you are working full-time in the summer or part-time after school, it's important to know that you are gaining valuable work skills with each job that you have regardless of the type of job. You are learning how to work with different people, how to conduct yourself in a professional work environment, and many other skills.

Your part-time work experience will help boost your college applications and for those students who choose to work right after high school, employers will consider your past work experience before offering you the job.

Regardless of where you work, while still in school your first job is getting an education and your work hours should allow time in your schedule to complete school work.

TEN WAYS TO FIND A JOB

Where should you start to look for a job?
There are literally tons of resources that can
help. Be patient, it may take some time. Your
persistence and consistency will pay off. Here
are a few tips to help you.

1. Talk to your friends who currently have
jobs and find out where they work and how
they got their job. Ask if their company
is hiring.

2. Let everyone know that you are looking for
a job.

3. Look through your local newspapers.

4. Walk around your neighborhood and
downtown area and look for buildings with
help wanted signs.

5. Ask your parents, siblings, and other
family members to ask around among their
friends to see who might be hiring.

6. Surf the Internet. Many companies post their job listings on their Web sites.

7. Talk to your school job counselor, teacher, or guidance counselor.

8. If you have a mentor, ask that person for help.

9. Go through your school's alumni network and conduct informational interviews with a few alumni and let them know you are looking.

10. Call your city's teen job hotline.

Bonus: Create your own job.

Finding a job is your responsibility. Don't sabotage your search by assuming others should know and will call you. Even though people are willing to help, it is up to you to remind them, pleasantly, that you are still looking. Remember be patient, persistent, and consistent.

CHAPTER TWO

APPLYING FOR A JOB

. Writing a Résumé

. Samples of a Résumé

. Preparing for a Job Interview

. Possible Interview Questions

WRITING A RÉSUMÉ

One of the basic tools in your job search is a résumé. Although some companies only require a completed application, many others expect you to have a résumé to get a job. A résumé is important. It is a professional representation of your work experience and can help employers get to know your skills and abilities.

There are many different ways to design a résumé. Visit your local library or school careers center for more ideas on résumé writing. Here are a few commonly asked questions about résumés.

Q. What exactly is a résumé?
A. A résumé is basically a history of your work experience with your current or most recent job listed first, then working backward; for each, tell where you worked, for how long, and what your responsibilities were, along with a telephone number. A résumé also includes other relevant information such as your education, community service work, extracurricular activities, related school

assignments or projects, prizes, certificates, awards, and special skills.

Q. I never had a job, what do I put on my résumé?
A. If you never had a job, you can still include all the other information listed above.

Q. How long is a résumé?
A. It's best to keep your résumé to one page only. If you have more, ask someone to help you get it to fit on one page. Try different fonts or adjust the size of the font. Use bullets instead of sentences. Be sure the spelling, grammar, and punctuation are all correct.

Q. Do I have to type my résumé?
A. Yes, of course. This is a professional document and it needs to look neat, clean, and legible. Avoid fancy fonts. I recommend Times New Roman or Arial, with a font size of 12 pt. On a Mac, Geneva works well and maybe a 10 pt is okay. Basically, it should be easy to read quickly.

<u>**Sample Résumé 1**</u>
Joe Money   617-555-4444
23 Greenback Drive
Success Town, MA 01010
E-mail: Iwantmoney@money.com

EDUCATION
Success High   Graduation Expected 2002

WORK EXPERIENCE
March 01-Present
Win Designs   617-505-2475
Cashier. Process all store purchases. Calculate
daily store revenue. Assist customers in making
clothing choices.

Summer 2000
Success Supermarket 617-535-1924
Grocery Bagger. Bag groceries, clean cash register
stations, assist customers and carry bags to car.

SCHOOL ACTIVITIES
Football Team 1998-2001
National Honor Society 2000-2001

SKILLS: Fluent Spanish, Data Entry

References provided upon request
Please note font reduced to this fit page

Sample Résumé 2
Monique Fashion
43 Runway Drive
ParisTown, MA 01010
617-444-5555
E-mail: lawyer@getjustice.com

EDUCATION
Success High   Graduation Expected 2003

Camp Reach High   Summer 2000
Counselor in Training (CIT)

COMMUNITY SERVICE   Sept. 00-Present
The Homeless Project   617-434-8381
Volunteer: Read weekly to homeless children.
Help serve food to families in the shelter.

EXTRACURRICULAR ACTIVITIES
Member of Debate Team   2000-2001

SKILLS
Build Web sites
Child care

References provided upon request

Please note font reduced to this fit page

PREPARING FOR A JOB INTERVIEW

You are getting ready for the job interview. What do you say? What kinds of questions will they ask? What if you make a mistake? Don't panic! Think of a job interview as a way for the employer to get to know you as a person and for you to convince them that you can do the job and are the best person to fill the position.

For your interview to be a success there are a few essentials that must be attended to before you begin answering questions. The tips that follow will help you make the best impression before, during, and after the interview.

Before the Interview

1. Know how to get to the interview location. If the address is unfamiliar take a trip to the general area a few days before the actual interview. Look for parking areas if you plan to drive or time your walking distance if you need to walk to the location.

2. Prepare a typed list of references and take three copies with you to the interview. Ask

three people who know you well (such as teachers or counselors at school, a former employer, or your religious leader) if you can give their names as references. On your list, give their name, title (if any), their phone number, and how they know you. Do not EVER give a reference without asking for permission first!

3. Research the company. Find out general information about the company: what kind of business it is, who are their customers, does it provide a service or produce a product for sale? Check the library, Web site, or call the Chamber of Commerce.

The Day of the Interview
1. Take three copies of your resume and three copies of your list of references, unfolded, in a clean, new folder or envelope. If you are not asked for them, offer one of each near the end of the interview.

2. Go to the interview alone. Do not take a friend or relative or have anyone meet you after the interview within the interview area

or the parking area. Meet or have them pick you up around the corner.

3. Arrive on time. It's okay to arrive about 5-10 minutes early, but NEVER arrive late. Arriving more than 10-15 minutes early can be an inconvenience to the interviewer.

4. Dress for work. Look professional, clean, and well groomed. Refer to Chapter Three for tips on personal grooming and dressing for the workplace.

During the Interview
1. Turn off your cell phone and beeper. You want to make a good first impression and a ringing phone or noisy beeper will not make you look important.

2. Remain calm and relaxed. You probably will be a little nervous, but try to breathe slowly to help calm the butterflies.

3. Address the interviewers by name. Unless you are given permission to use a person's first name, be respectful and use a title (Mr. or Ms) and last name when addressing them.

4. Avoid fidgeting. It's distracting and makes you appear less confident. See the section titled Body Talk in Chapter Six.

5. Answer questions honestly. Lying or exaggerating when answering questions will only reflect badly on your character, especially if your references say something different, or if you are hired and the interviewer finds you out later.

6. Be brief and precise when answering questions. Providing lengthy answers, giving irrelevant information, or answering questions in one word ("yes" or "no") will not present a professional image of you. Instead say "No, I don't have any experience doing that," or "Yes, I can start on Monday."

7. Have at least three prepared questions. As the interview draws to a close, the interviewer will probably ask you if you have any questions. Never say "No, I do not have any questions." Always come prepared with at least three questions to ask. Some examples might be: "What is your dress code for my job?" "What kind of training and orientation do you

provide?" "What do you think is the most important factor for me to do a good job for you?"

8. Ask for the interviewer's business card. If at the end the interview, the interviewer has not offered you a card, politely ask for one. "May I please have one of your cards?"

After the Interview
1. Send a thank you note. Within one week of the interview, write a note saying thanks for taking the time to meet with you; include your contact information.

2. Wait to hear from the interviewer. Be patient and wait to hear if you've been hired. If you have not heard after two weeks, give the interviewer a call and politely ask when they expect to make a decision.

POSSIBLE INTERVIEW QUESTIONS

The interviewer will decide if you will be the best candidate for the job by the way you answer the interview questions. You should have a list of questions to ask the employer to make sure that this is the kind of company you want to work for. All employers want the people who work for them to be able to present themselves professionally, be reliable, responsible, honest, and hard working. These expectations are the same if you are filing in an office building or flipping burgers at the local fast food restaurant.

The following questions are typical interview questions. Look through these questions and think about how you would answer each one.

1. Tell me about yourself?

2. What are three strengths you possess?

3. What are three of your weaknesses? This one is tough. Don't put yourself down. Instead of saying "I am always late getting work done," say (if it's true) "I am a

perfectionist and sometimes need more time to complete the work."

4. Why do you want to work for this company?

5. Why should we hire you?

6. Why did you leave your last job?
This is a tough one, too. Never put down your former job or employer. Say something neutral like "I want to try a different kind of work," or "It just wasn't something I felt I could be good at."

7. What are your dreams and goals?

8. What was the last book you read?

9. When can you start?

10. Do you have any questions for me?

CHAPTER THREE

DRESSING FOR WORK

. But I Do Look Good

. Appropriate Dress for
Young Women

. Appropriate Dress for
Young Men

. Casual Fridays

. The 411 on Accessories

. The "Do" on Hairdos

. Ten Tips on Personal Grooming

. Dressing Your Personality
for Success

BUT I DO LOOK GOOD

Why should employers care about how you look as long as you get the work done? This is a common sentiment expressed by many teenagers. Let's look at it.

When your favorite sports team comes out on the field they are dressed for the sport. Think of basketball, football, or soccer players: you never see any of them coming out onto the field or playing floor in a tie and dress shoes, or a hockey player on the ice with a tank top and sneakers.

The same is true in the business world. Although many businesses do not wear uniforms and the technology industry has a more relaxed dress code, each workplace has a standard of dress that is expected in order to maintain a sense of professionalism. If you plan to work in that environment you need to follow the rules.

Professional clothing is expensive, but you do not need to spend a fortune to look professional and you do not have to buy brand name clothing. Quality, moderate price, non-brand name professional clothing can be bought at a fraction of what some teenagers pay for designer clothing and sneakers. Check your local department store and compare prices.

When shopping for clothing, here are a few guidelines that can help you choose the most appropriate attire. The descriptions that follow assume you will be working in a work environment that prefers traditional work attire.

NOTE: If your job is of a physical nature, if you are working outdoors in dirty areas, or in retail, food service or health your dress code may be different. Check with your company for policies on dress codes.

APPROPRIATE DRESS FOR
YOUNG WOMEN

\# Skirts. Should be no more than 2" above the knee. Choose material that does not cling to your body (i.e., spandex).

\# Blouse or shirt. Go for a loose (not baggy) fit. Ensure that neck lines do not expose any part of your cleavage.

\# Jacket. A professional jacket flows past the waist area and ends mid-hip.

\# Turtleneck. Should be worn under a sweater or jacket, not by itself.

\# Sweaters. Some sweaters are appropriate if they are not close fitting or glittering material and not studded with sparkles or fake rhinestones.

\# Dress pants. Look for loose fitting (not baggy) pants that flow to the ankle. Make sure your pants do not drag on the floor. No jeans unless specifically permitted by the company.

\# Scarfs. Use to dress up your outfits.

Clothing to Avoid for Young Women

\# Tight jeans, skirts, sweaters, blouses, or dresses.

\# Skirts or dresses with long slits that expose the thigh; slits should stop at the knee.

\# Skirts made from light material where undergarment or body outline is easily recognized.

\# Midriffs, halters, or tank tops.

\# Micro mini skirts.

APPROPRIATE DRESS FOR
YOUNG MEN

^ Dress shirt. Button down the front, long or short sleeves. Solid colors in a cotton or polyester with a collar so you can wear a tie.

^ Dress pants. Khakis are often a good example of dress pants. Slacks or suit pants are too. Pants should be worn on the waist with a belt. No jeans unless specifically permitted by the company.

^ Dress shoes. Usually leather or leather looking and requires a regular shine.

^ Jackets. A sport coat or suit jacket is often optional for young men.

^ Ties. Every young man should have at least three ties. Have fun when choosing ties and have at least one that is conservative.

^ Turtlenecks. They are great under jackets or sweaters.

^ Sweaters. Choose simple, clean-cut designs without wild patterns or colors.

Clothing to Avoid for Young Men

^ Lumberjack shirts.
^ Muscle shirts.
^ Baggy pants that fall below the waistline
    and drag on the floor.
^ Exposed underwear.
^ Baseball caps.

Clothing to Avoid for Both Men and Women

~ Shorts.
~ Sneakers (depending on your job).
~ Hiking boots.
~ Clothes with offensive language or images.
~ Fashionably torn clothing.
~ Sweat pants or sweat shirts.
~ Hats.
~ Shiny, party clothing (glitters, neon, etc.).
~ Tee shirts.

CASUAL FRIDAYS

Many companies have adopted a casual Friday policy. That does not mean you can now wear whatever you like. Workers who normally dress in suits all week are able to wear more relaxed attire such as sport jackets with a turtleneck and women can dress down a bit without a formal business suit.

Since most teenagers do not dress in suits on a regular basis when they work, the clothing outlined in the previous pages is still the best on casual Fridays. Young men can probably choose not to wear a tie, and clean jeans, not ragged, not patched, preferably black, may be acceptable. All the clothing in the section about clothing to avoid is still to be avoided even on casual Fridays.

THE 411 ON ACCESSORIES

Your accessories are a demonstration of your sense of style. Earrings, body rings, beaded jewelry help make you different or a part of the crowd. However, a few tips can help you develop a new sense of style geared towards the workplace. It need not be for 24 hours a day, but it will help you look professional at work. Here are answers to commonly asked questions.

Q. How many earrings can I wear?
A. No more than two earrings.

Q. How many rings can I wear?
A. Keep rings to a minimum, 2-3 max.

Q. Why does it matter how many bracelets I wear?
A. They may not always see them, but chances are if you are wearing multiple bracelets they can hear them and it's distracting.

Q. Can I wear my rings and studs in other pierced body parts?
A. Not unless you are working in an environment where your accessories can actually help business, a body piercing shop for example.

Q. Why does the size of my jewelry matter?
A. Oversize pieces of jewelry are attention grabbers, especially large linked chains and flashy rings. You are in a job to work, not to be a fashion statement.

Q. Why can't I wear designer nails?
A. Nail shops have become creative with their designs, but fancy designs with studs, tropical scenes, and loud colors are not appropriate for work. Wear natural or soft color nail polish. French tips are acceptable.

Q. Does the size of my purse matter?
A. Yes, it does. If you are going to an interview, women should carry a small or medium size purse. Bulky bags (especially shopping bags) or backpacks are too cumbersome and unprofessional.

Q. Why is the way I wear my make-up so important?

A. Some teenage girls tend to overdo their makeup. Your make-up should be a soft way to enhance your natural beauty, not create a new you. Heavy foundation, bright or very dark colored lipsticks, black outlined lips, too much blush, and extra dark eyebrows are some of the common make-up mistakes young women make when preparing for work.

Q. What about perfumes and after shave?

A. Stick with light fragrances and wear in small doses. Many people have allergies to certain fragrances. Be sensitive to your coworkers' needs.

THE "DO" ON HAIRDOS

Your hairstyle is another way you express your sense of style. However, since your goal is to get a job and keep it, it's important to understand that this is another area where there are unspoken rules.

Young Women
1. Stay with natural human hair colors. Bright reds or varying shades of neon colors are not appropriate for a traditional work environment, but might be okay for the music industry, or if you wear hats all day long.

2. Avoid trendy hairstyles that are designed to be attention grabbers with spray-on glitters, or spiked upwards or outward.

3. Braided extensions should be clean and neat at all times.

Young Men
1. Braids, dreads, and the no-comb hairstyles are unacceptable in the traditional workforce.
2. Young men need to cut their hair regularly.
3. Low-cuts are preferred, no styling gel.

TEN PERSONAL GROOMING TIPS

Here are a few personal grooming tips that will help you look polished and project a professional image.

1. Select your outfit the night before.
2. Check to make sure all outfits are clean, unstained, and well pressed, have all the buttons, and no split seams.
3. Make sure your shoes are comfortable.
4. Clean your shoes, no scuff marks.
5. Buy, and carry with you, an extra pair of panty hose in case they run.
6. Shower daily and don't forget deodorant.
7. Clean and trim your nails.
8. No gum chewing. Freshen-up with mints.
9. Brush your teeth daily.
10. No smoking.

DRESSING YOUR PERSONALITY
FOR SUCCESS

You are not totally dressed until you dress
your personality. How do you dress
your personality?

1. Have a positive attitude.
2. Smile.
3. Show enthusiasm.
4. Talk less, listen more.
5. Shake hands firmly.
6. Remember the names of people you meet.
7. Imagine positive outcomes.
8. Volunteer.
9. Make eye contact.
10. Treat others in a fair manner always.

CHAPTER FOUR

TIME IS MONEY

. Time Savers and Time Wasters

. On-the-Job Time Management

TIME SAVERS AND TIME WASTERS

Your life is busy. Time is spent at school, with family and friends, and at work. Time is even more precious for seniors applying to college and for teens who are also parents. With such demands, good choices must be made about how your time is spent.

Time management is less about time itself and more about decision-making. Good decisions make it easier to manage your schedule and stay in control, so you can maximize the 24 hours that we all have each day. When you make hasty or unplanned decisions there are often unwanted consequences.

You are the one in control of your 24 hours and no one else. You get the credit for your choices. Likewise, if you choose not to accept that responsibility and use your time unwisely, you cannot blame others for the results.

Time Savers

~ Use a personal calendar.
It does not matter whether it's on your computer, in a palm pilot, or in an appointment book. Record appointments, due dates for projects, and important commitments to help you stay in control.

~ Plan carefully.
Always estimate the amount of time a project or task will take to complete, then add in extra time for unforeseen circumstances that may cause delays.

~ Ask for help.
Smart people are the ones who recognize when they are unable to deliver by themselves and recruit others to assist.

~ Call ahead.
A quick phone call can save trips and time.

~ Set priorities.
Make choices and decisions based on your future goals rather than the spur of the moment.

Time Wasters

~ Worry.
More time is often spent worrying, stressing, and complaining about doing something than the actual time it will take to complete the task.

~ Over committing yourself.
It's hard to say "no" when a friend needs your help. Your time is very valuable and it is unfair to yourself to spread yourself thin and become overwhelmed by doing favors for others. Be selective and know when to say "no."

~ Chatting on the phone/surfing the Internet.
No teenager can function well without staying in touch with friends locally and internationally. However, as you chat the days away, remember you also have a future coming up!

~ Procrastination.
This behavior is best described as putting off doing something by any possible means or excuses. Stop sabotaging yourself.

~ Love sickness

Hearts are being broken and hearts are falling in love all the time. A lot of time is spent preoccupied daydreaming about the other person. Keep an eye on your goals, too!

ON-THE-JOB TIME MANAGEMENT

One of the biggest differences between school and the workplace is the concept of time. In the work world everything seems to be measured by time. It's the old saying "Time is money." With that in mind there are a few points that most companies would like for all employees to understand. Mastering time management now will help you stand out as an exemplary student and employee. The following are common questions about time and the workplace.

Q. How can I be late for work, if I'm in the building or in my work area?
A. The workday begins when you start working not when you enter the building or the general work area. If you like to get refreshments before you begin to work, arrive early, so you can get them and still begin on time.

Q. I have a legitimate excuse why I'm late for work, the train is always late and when I drive traffic is backed up. Why is my supervisor still making this a big deal?
A. Having an excuse for being late does not

make everything okay. Part of the responsibility of being a good worker is to plan extra time in your travel schedule to accommodate unforeseen events when they occur, so you can still arrive early.

Q. Why do I have to call, if I'm only going to be a few minutes late?
A. It's the courteous, responsible thing to do. It lets your coworkers know how to reschedule their work, if necessary.

Q. I call when I'm going to be late, but that does not seem to satisfy the people I work with. What should I do?
A. It's important that you call. However, when you are late other people in your department or on your shift may have to wait for you before starting their own work. If you are relieving someone, you are holding him or her up. Make an extra effort to arrive on time consistently, so when you do call coworkers may be more willing to understand.

Q. If I'm done with all my work, is it okay to leave a few minutes early?
A. No. It's great that you are able to complete all your work, however, you need to honor the time for which you are being paid. Do not start doing homework or ask your supervisor to leave early. Instead ask for more work, assist a coworker, or take the time to prepare for the next workday.

Q. I'm bored out of my mind and my supervisor is not giving me anything to do. She is always busy or not in the office. What should I do?
A. It can be frustrating if you have nothing to do and everyone else seems busy. Resist the urge to fall asleep or be unproductive. Approach your supervisor, if that person is in the area, or leave a note, e-mail, or voice mail and let that person know that you would like to work. In the mean time, check with coworkers and see whether you can help them. You will be showing that you are ambitious and not afraid to take the initiative to get the most out of your work experience.

Q. Is it okay to spend a few extra minutes at lunch especially since other people in the department do it?

A. No. It is not okay. When you do that you are cheating the company out of its time because you still expect them to pay you even though you were not working. You are laying the foundations and setting your personal standards for your future work life even if you feel your job now is insignificant.

Q. If I meet my friend during a quick run to the bathroom, why can't I stand and talk for a little while?

A. It's okay to meet fellow coworkers and friends during a break and exchange a few words, but it is not acceptable if you stop to have mini-marathon conversations when you are getting paid for working.

CHAPTER FIVE

TELECOMMUNICATIONS

. Telephone Skills

. Internet Skills

. Fax Skills

TELEPHONE SKILLS

It's no secret that most teenagers love to talk on the phone. At times it seems like you would probably die if you did not have a phone. But the rules for phone usage on the job and at home are very different. Here are a few quick tips that will help you understand phone usage in the workplace.

 # Use the phone for business purposes only.
Although some companies may not be concerned over an occasional personal call, it's best not to make personal calls on the company phone or on company time. Be aware that many companies do monitor their phone system.

 # Take proper phone messages.
Most companies now have voice mail, but you may be asked to take a message manually. In such an event make sure you have all the following information: name of the person who will receive the message, the name of the caller, phone number of the caller, date and time of message, the actual message and your

name and extension as the person taking the message. Remember to deliver the message.

Be voice mail friendly.
When leaving a message make sure to speak slowly, clearly, leave your name and phone number, and a good time to call you back.

No beepers and cell phones allowed.
Company issued beepers or cell phones are fine for the workplace. However, personal beepers and cell phones should be turned off during work hours. Check your messages during lunch or break periods.

Answer the phone professionally.
Ask your supervisor about the preferred way to answer the phone. Most companies want you to identify yourself, the department, and/or the company name.

Keep it clear, concise, and cheerful.
Studies show that teenagers need to sleep more than the average person, but it's important not to sound sleepy when answering the phone; be cheerful even at 9 am on a summer morning.

Ask before you hit the "hold" button.
Saying, "hold please" is not asking. Instead ask, "May I please put you on hold?" and wait for a reply before you put someone on hold. Then don't forget about the call on hold!

Learn to transfer calls.
We've all lost a call trying to transfer it. Learn how to use your company's systems, so callers don't get lost in the phone system or fall deaf when you touch tone the numbers while they are on the line.

No personal calls, please.
Personal calls should be made on your own time. It's best not to use the company phone, use the pay phone or your own cell phone.

Pick up that ringing phone.
If you are allowed to answer the phones try to pick up the call by the third ring. Sometimes that may not be possible. However, it is best to strive for such excellence, as the caller will appreciate your promptness and you will establish good habits for your future career.

INTERNET SKILLS

As enticing as the Internet can be, it's best to think twice about using the Internet or intranet in your workplace for personal e-mail or activities. Once again, you are being paid to do company work.

^ Use the Internet for work purposes, only.
Resist the urge to check your personal e-mail during work hours. Research should be work related, not for homework and school research papers.

^ Use proper English.
Even though Internet language has shortened phrases, please use proper English when sending e-mails to anyone in the company. Reread your e-mails and do spelling and grammar checks before sending.

^ No chain letters.
Do not forward chain letters, jokes, and stories to coworkers. It is a time waster and clogs up other workers' e-mail.

^ Know the rules.
Typing e-mails in all CAPITAL LETTERS is considered rude and is equivalent to yelling. Sending unsolicited e-mails or spam is a violation of cyber rules.

^ Fill in the blanks.
Complete the subject line in e-mails, give the proper salutations "Dear…" and remember to include your e-mail signature (name, department, company, and phone number).

^ Avoid interoffice personal e-mail.
Don't e-mail personal friends who work in the same company. Work is not the time to make plans with friends or find out how they are doing.

FAX SKILLS

When you are responsible for sending faxes or delivering incoming faxes to the appropriate recipients, here's how you can do a great job with this responsibility.

~ Always use a cover sheet.
Fax cover sheets should be used with every fax, and include the sender's name, fax and phone numbers; the recipient's name, phone and fax numbers; and the number of pages being sent. All companies have a standard fax cover sheet.

~ Learn to use the fax machine.
Ask your supervisor or coworker to show you how to use the fax machine correctly.

~ Ask for help when it's broken.
Notify the appropriate person when the fax malfunctions. Do not be afraid, chances are it wasn't your fault and all that's needed could be minor maintenance.

CHAPTER SIX

PEOPLE SKILLS

. Working with Your Supervisor

. Interacting with Coworkers

. Body Talk

. Listening 101

. Problem Solving Skills

. Language Skills

WORKING WITH YOUR SUPERVISOR

Supervisors are in charge because the company has confidence in their ability to perform supervisory responsibilities and get the results the company needs to make a profit. A supervisor's role is to guide employees to become the best worker each can be by developing their skills. This is not always easy, but every employee needs to know how to work with his or her supervisor and build a professional relationship. You do not have to be best friends with your supervisor, but to keep your job, relate to your supervisor with respectful courtesy. You can learn a lot!

1. Be willing to learn.
Show your supervisor that you are eager to learn, to try new things, and do extra tasks.

2. Be proactive.
Whenever there is a problem, immediately notify your supervisor if you are not able to resolve the issue. Don't waste time on it.

3. Speak up.

Some jobs that teenagers do are quite boring, but are absolutely essential to the company. Ask your supervisor to vary the tasks that you do and try to identify areas you would like to learn more about.

4. Understand the company.

Learn how your daily responsibilities help the company; this helps you to become a better employee and work well with your supervisor.

5. Ask for clarification.

Always ask questions when in doubt. Do not feel intimidated or shy. It's better to ask many questions and do a task well than to guess what is wanted and make errors.

6. Follow directions.

It sounds simple, but it can be difficult. Employee and supervisor relationships are more productive when an employee can follow instructions from the supervisor.

7. Be innovative.

Look for ways to improve the processes in your area and share those with your supervisor, but don't make changes without first getting approval to go ahead.

INTERACTING WITH COWORKERS

Chances are you will not be working by yourself all the time. Therefore, it is critical that
you develop your people skills and foster
professional relationships with coworkers
based on respect.

Respect is earned as relationships develop and
people get to know each other. Always show
respect to others even when they may be
disrespectful to you. This will demonstrate
your maturity and your respect for yourself.

Keep personal business private.
It's difficult not to show feelings and
emotions. However, in a workplace setting
whether it's retail, the supermarket, a shop, or
an office, try not to make your personal life a
topic of discussion.

Keep it clean.
Not many people like to clean up. If you've
been assigned a workstation, keep it clean
and organized.

Respect your coworker's space.
In the event you need to use a coworker's workspace keep it clean and neat, and do not rummage through the desk or lockers.

Smile please.
Even when it's been a hard day and life seems impossible, try to smile and be a welcoming face to those around you.

"Please" and "thank you."
These little words are critical. People judge you positively or negatively when you use them and when you don't. Use them often.

Listen to your tone of voice.
The tone of voice you use when speaking with others is determined by how you feel at that moment when addressing someone. Anger, frustration, or sarcasm are easily detected. Be aware of this while speaking.

Good jokes are really funny.
Jokes that are harsh, discriminating, or in questionable taste should not be told. They are offensive and can cause discord in workplaces. If coworkers are telling these

jokes walk away and do not encourage or laugh with them.

Know your limit.
It's easy to be influenced by adults or other teens on the job. Learn from responsible workers and never imitate coworkers who break company policies, no matter how small.

Own your mistakes.
All humans make mistakes. Honest, mature teens own their mistakes and bear the consequences, if there are any.

Limit socializing.
Casually visiting coworkers at their work areas should not become a habit. It is a distraction and interrupts the workflow.

BODY TALK

Yes, your body talks and people pay more attention to your body language than the actual words you say. There is an old saying "Your actions speak so loud, I can't hear what you are saying." Let your words and body say the same thing!

Be mindful of what your body is communicating to those around you, as there are both positive and negative body languages.

Negative Body Language
The following are perceived as negative body signals that communicate nervousness, insecurity, frustration, anger, or defensiveness: head shake, eyes roll up with a shrug, crossed arms, sideways glances, checking the time, frowning, fidgeting, biting fingernails, chewing pens or pencils, hissing, pointing a finger, and tapping or twitching a foot.

Positive Body Language
The following signals are positive body language that presents you as a person of confidence, cooperation, and openness:

standing tall; sitting up straight; chin up; smile; steeple, upturned, or open hands; hands behind your back when standing; and lean forward and tilt head toward speaker.

Learn to Shake Hands
There is an art to shaking hands. Offer your right hand, give a brief squeeze, and hold for a second. It says that you are confident and not aggressive.

LISTENING 101

There is a technique to listening. Normally
when people speak, it is so easy not to listen
to the other person. We are preoccupied
trying to figure out how to respond and get
our point across.

Having good listening skills will help you as
an individual interact better with others as
you learn to listen to spoken words and what
is not said. If you want to make a good
impression, just close your mouth and open
your ears. You'll be amazed at what you will
learn. Practice your listening skills often.
Good listeners do the following:

~ **Maintain eye contact.**
Do not stare, but do look at the person to
whom you are speaking, glance away once in
a while, then look back. This indicates your
interest and respect for that person.

~ **Show interest.**
Nod your head, say words like "Ah ha," "I
see," "Really," and "Okay." These all indicate
to the speaker that you're listening.

~ Do not interrupt.

Allow the speaker time to finish his/her thoughts before you begin to speak.

~ Paraphrase what you understand.

Repeat back to the speaker what you heard. Start off by saying something like, "Did I hear you correctly..." then repeat what you understood and allow the speaker to correct you if you misunderstood some information. Even if you didn't get it exactly right, the speaker will feel good that you tried to really understand.

PROBLEM SOLVING SKILLS

Resolving problems quickly and in a sensible way is essential at school and also in the workplace. Small concerns can balloon into big issues when the right problem solving techniques are not applied.

Here are a few ways to look at problems and come up with solutions quickly and safely.

1. When someone offends you try not to loose your temper. Walk away, calm down, and think about how you would like to approach the person. It must be a calm conversation.

2. Talk over the problem with a neutral adult to brainstorm ways to resolve the issue.

3. Never try to resolve a problem when you are angry, frustrated, or tired. Take a break, get rested, then come back to it. Don't try to ignore it or forget, as it could happen again if it is not resolved the first time.

4. Think about the results you want. It is difficult to vow never to speak to a coworker again. Be sensible and make sound decisions.

5. Violence, cursing, verbal abuse, or getting even are never options.

LANGUAGE SKILLS

Teens have a language all to themselves, but proper English is expected in the workplace. Slang or broken English is inappropriate for the workplace, even though it may be okay in other settings.

^ Profanity is an absolute "No, No!"

^ Derogatory words, demeaning gestures, and racial or religious slurs are not ever acceptable at work.

^ Listen to how others around you speak, preferably those in authority. Most times they provide a good example to follow.

^ Talk to an English teacher and practice speaking proper English whether English is your first or second language.

CHAPTER SEVEN

CUSTOMER SERVICE

. Making Customers Happy

. When Customers Make You Mad

MAKING CUSTOMERS HAPPY

"Our customers are number one." "The customer is always right." These are slogans that many companies have adopted. What does that mean for you as a worker?

Many teenagers have jobs dealing directly with customers and pleasing the customer is crucial for any business to stay open. The way a customer is treated will determine if he/she will come back again. Repeat clients are what make a company profitable.

What makes a customer happy?

Call them by name.
If you know the customer's name, use it. It makes them feel special. If you do not know their name, address the customer as "Sir," or "Ma'am."

Acknowledge customers immediately.
Greet customers as soon as they enter by saying "hello," "welcome," "good morning," "good evening," or "be right with you." If unable to verbally communicate at the

moment, use body language, smiles, or hand
signals to acknowledge them.

Listen to customers
Almost everyone craves undivided attention.
Listen with your body or if on the phone give
verbal affirmations (see section on Listening
101 in Chapter Six).

Be flexible.
Know your company's policies. Know also
that some customers may require a bit more to
please them; it's called going the extra mile.

Say "Thank you and have a nice day!"
Again, make each customer feel special. Let
them see that you do appreciate them.

Understand the customer profile.
Customers have habits and needs that make
them shop in different places. When you
understand them it's easier to make them feel
like number one. You will then be able to
anticipate and meet their needs before they
even ask.

WHEN CUSTOMERS MAKE YOU MAD

Is the customer really always right? No, the customer is not really always right, but the company wants customers to feel special. Not every customer is wonderful to serve. Some people are just hard to please; they complain and seem to be always in a bad mood.

Sometimes the company is to blame because the policies do not meet the needs of the customer. Sometimes another employee has been rude to the customer. The mark of a true professional, adult or teenager, is how that difficult customer is treated. What techniques can you use to please this type of customer?

Stay calm.
They may not be angry with you. More than likely it's the company and its policies, not you personally. Be aware of your attitude and remain positive.

Be patient.
Listen to their complaints with your body, voice, and imagination to hear their real needs.

Apologize quickly.
Customers just want companies to take responsibility. Saying "I'm sorry" helps the customers feel better. Be genuine in your apology, even if you are not, personally, to blame. You are speaking for the company.

Help them.
Fix their problem if you can. That's all most upset customers want.

Never argue with customers.
Even when you know they are wrong, never argue with customers. It proves nothing, no one really wins, and your supervisor could bring disciplinary actions against you.

Refer to your supervisor.
When you are unable to assist a customer ask someone with more authority or knowledge, like a supervisor or coworker, to help resolve the issue.

CHAPTER EIGHT

JUSTICE ON THE JOB

. Your Legal Rights

. Sexual Harassment

. Drug Testing in the Workplace

YOUR LEGAL RIGHTS

As a working teenager, you need to know that there are government rules that are designed to protect you on the job. These rules cover the number of hours you are allowed to work, what kinds of jobs you can have, and your employer's obligation to provide a safe environment in which to work. Here are general answers to commonly asked questions. Each state can set its own rules, so it is always wise to check for specific information for your state.

Q. How old do I have to be to get a job?
A. In most states, 14 and 15 year olds are allowed to work, but on a limited basis.

Q. Are there any jobs for youths under 14?
A. Yes, you can work as a newspaper carrier, entertainer, perform domestic work (baby-sitting, party help, yard care), a golf course caddie, or if you are at least 12 years old you can work on a farm.

Q. Do I have to have a work permit if I'm 14 or 15?
A. Many states require 14 and 15 year olds to obtain "working papers," also called a "work permit," before they begin working. Check with your school counselors or Department of Labor as some states also require a signed letter from your doctor before you can begin working.

Q. How many hours can I work if I'm 14 or 15?
A. <u>During the school year:</u>
   3 hours per day, 18 hours a week,
   7 a.m. - 7 p.m., not during school hours
<u>On Weekends:</u>
   8 hours per day weekends and holidays
<u>During the summer:</u>
   8 hours per day, 40 hours per week

Q. Can my school stop me from working if I do not keep my grades up?
A. Yes. If you are working because you received a working permit or working papers, the counselor who issued the permit can revoke your right to work until your grades improve.

Q. I'm 16 . What hours can I work?
A. Some states have restrictions on the number of hours 16 and 17 year olds can work. Check with your school about your individual state.

Q. Are there jobs I cannot get?
A. If you are under 18 years old, you can not work in jobs considered to be dangerous such as manufacturing, driving vehicles, storing of explosives, logging, roofing, excavation, wrecking, demolition, slaughtering, meat-packing, and meat processing.

Also, you are not allowed to operate, clean, set up, adjust, or repair any of the following: food slicers, grinders, choppers, cutters, and com-mercial mixers. Power machinery such as saws (all types), hoisting equipment, guillo-tine shears, and metal forming machinery fall under this category as well.

Q. What should I do if my supervisor asks me to perform a dangerous, hazardous task?
A. Calmly remind your supervisor that because of your age you are not allowed to perform such duties. If the incident occurs

again, report it to the Human Resources office, a parent, school counselor, or trusted adult.

Q. Do these rules apply when I am in a vocational education program?
A. Students in vocational educational programs who are expected to work with machinery or under conditions deemed hazardous or dangerous need to check with school officials for specific guidelines that govern apprenticeships.

Q. How much am I supposed to be paid?
A. Federal law states that your starting wage must be at least the current minimum wage.

Q. How much is overtime pay?
A. People who work over 40 hours are eligible for overtime. Overtime, or time and a half, means you will be paid 1.5 times your hourly wage. If your regular hourly wage is $6 an hour, then you will receive $9 per hour for each overtime hour worked.

SEXUAL HARASSMENT

One area of workplace behavior teens must understand in order to be successful is sexual harassment. Some school environments tend not to be as strict as workplaces even though sexual harassment policies are in place. Teenagers often do not address sexual harassment as they do not want to stand out in the crowd or be labeled a tattletale.

Q. What is sexual harassment?
A. It is unwelcome sexual advances, requests for sexual favors, verbal statements, or physical contacts that are of a sexual nature, or displaying objects or pictures that are sexually suggestive.

Q. Can boys be sexually harassed?
A. Yes. Sexual harassment affects men and women, boys and girls.

Q. Is sexual harassment only between persons of the opposite sex?
A. No. Sexual harassment can also occur female to female or male to male.

Q. What should I do if I think I've been sexually harassed?

A. Report the incident to a supervisor immediately, and also be sure to ask a parent, teacher, or trusted adult to support you.

Q. What should I do if my supervisor is the offender?

A. Report the incident to the Human Resources offices immediately, and also be sure to ask a parent, teacher, or trusted adult to support you.

Q. When should I report incidents of sexual harassment?

A. Immediately. Do not wait, and also be sure to ask a parent, teacher, or trusted adult to support you.

Q. Is flirting sexual harassment?

A. It can only be classified as sexual harassment if the person you have an interest in considers this behavior unwanted and unwelcome.

Q. How do I know if the person does not like my behavior?

A. You can always ask. The person can let you know verbally, or with her or his body language. When you are told "no," you must accept it, even if you don't believe it.

Q. Can I be fired if I tell?

A. No. The law is designed to protect your job. If you are the victim, you should not be penalized for exercising your right to protect yourself.

DRUG TESTING IN THE WORKPLACE

Some employers may require that you take a
drug test when applying for work. This is
legal, as companies need to protect themselves
to insure all employees are coherent enough to
perform their jobs without putting themselves,
the company, or other employees at risk.

Q. What kind of test is utilized?
A. There are generally two types: the urine
test and the hair sample. The urine test is
more common. You may be asked to give a
urine sample and that is usually tested for
marijuana, or you could be asked for a hair
sample and that can be tested for marijuana as
well as other drugs.

Q. What do I need to bring to the test?
A. If you are under 18 years old, you must
provide a parental consent form before being
tested. Everyone is required to provide a
picture ID.

You will need to fill out a medical questionnaire, be sure to answer ALL questions, do
not leave any questions unanswered. Ask an

adult for help if you are unsure how to answer a question.

Q. What if I'm on medication?
A. If you are on any kind of medication or you've taken any kind of over the counter medicine, including all painkillers, you should indicate that on the medical questionnaire you fill out before taking the test.

Q. If I am around people who smoke marijuana can I test positive even though I was not smoking?
A. There is a possibility that you may test positive depending on your metabolism. If you inhale smoke from marijuana cigarettes you may test positive.

Q. What happens if I fail the drug test?
A. You will be denied employment. You will fail a drug test if your sample is positive for any illegal substances.

Q. How long do drugs stay in your system?
A. That depends on your body type, your weight, height, and body metabolism. Don't depend on taking substances that promise to clean all traces of drugs from your system, if you really want a job.

CHAPTER NINE

MONEY MATTERS

. Understanding your Paycheck

. Managing a Checking Account

. Using a Credit Card

. Saving and Investing Your Money

UNDERSTANDING YOUR PAYCHECK

It's wonderful to see the faces of teenagers when they get their first paycheck. It goes from excited to utter disbelief and confusion. This expression comes as you try to figure out the deductions and calculate the amount of hours worked and how much you are supposed to receive. To help ease some of that confusion here are a few tips.

Q. Who withholds money from my check and why?
A. The employer does for the government. Money can be taken out for your half of the Social Security and Medicare taxes known as the Federal Insurance Contributions Act (FICA), and for state and federal income taxes.

Q. How do I know what I am being paid?
A. You need to know before you start working what your hourly rate will be, and whether you're eligible for overtime. Multiply the number of hours worked times your hourly rate (calculate overtime hours separately), and that is the amount due to you (before withholding).

Q. How often do I get paid?
A. That depends on the company you work for. Most companies pay biweekly and some pay weekly. Ask your supervisor what schedule your company uses.

Q. What should I do if there is an error in my check?
A. Approach your supervisor in a CALM manner, state your case and ask him/her to help you figure out the error. To avoid problems, copy your time sheet every week and keep accurate records. If you punch a clock, have a book and keep track of all your hours, so you will have a back up record to help support your case if an error occurs.

Q. Do I have to file taxes?
A. Students are usually exempt from filing taxes because they do not make a significant amount of money. However, some students earn over the limit and will need to file. Talk with the person who prepares your family taxes or a school career counselor.

MANAGING A CHECKING ACCOUNT

As soon as you get your first check, choose a local bank and open both savings and checking accounts. You need a checking account, as it is not wise to carry large sums of cash. There are different types of checking accounts, shop around the different banks, and credit unions if you are eligible, and see which one has the type of account that is best for you. Here are a few hints:

No minimum balance. Find an account that does not require a minimum balance. This is important as some banks and credit unions charge a fee if you do not maintain a certain balance.

Overdraft protection. Get an account with an overdraft protection package as part of your checking account. In the event you have insufficient funds in your checking account, the bank will automatically go to your overdraft protection account (usually a savings account) to deduct funds to cover the transaction.

Get a debit card. A debit card is like a credit card, but you can only charge up to the amount of money in your account. It's very convenient and they come with a credit card logo, so no one knows the difference.

Ask about fees. There are fees to check balances by phone, by computer, ATM fees at your bank or if you use another bank's ATM machine, fee for insufficient funds if you are overdrawn, fees for bounced checks you receive, fees for paying bills online, and the list can go on.

Transaction limitations. Some banks have limitations on the number of transactions you can make before being charged a fee such as number of checks allowed monthly or number of debit card transactions. Know what they are and manage wisely.

Balancing your checkbook. If you know how to balance a checkbook, keeping your finances in order as an adult will be much easier. Get a head start now.

1. Record the opening balance for the account. This is the amount of money in your initial deposit. Remember to enter the fee for ordering checks.

2. Record all checks. Before you tear a check from the check book always record the transaction in the check register, the amount of the check, to whom the check is written, the number of the check, and the date the check was written, then calculate the new balance.

3. Record all deposits. As soon as you make a deposit, record that in the addition column of the checkbook then calculate the new balance. Keep the deposit slip in your records.

4. Subtract fees. If your bank charges fees for ATM transactions, and other types of fees be sure to subtract those as well.

5. Add the interest rate. The interest rates for checking accounts are usually very low but you still need to add the interest rate to balance your account. The easiest way to do this is when you get your monthly statement.

6. Balance your monthly statement. At the end of each month, it's important to check your statement for accuracy. Check off the checks that have been cashed and remember that sometimes even though you have written a check it takes a few days to register in your account. Make sure you have the same balance as the bank for the items on the statement.

7. Trouble shooting your account. In the event your checkbook does not balance, double check all transactions and ensure you deducted all fees, checks, and ATM transactions, and added interest rates. The bank will charge a fee so use that only as a last resort. That is still cheaper than ruining your credit record by being overdrawn.

USING A CREDIT CARD

There are advertisements everywhere sending messages that once you have a credit card, you will have no worries, the sky is the limit, and you can have a great time with family and friends. Having a credit card is not a right; it is a privilege that should be handled responsibly for there are serious long-term consequences when credit cards are mismanaged. When you obtain a credit card you are agreeing with the credit card company to pay back in full all the debt you borrow.

Getting a Credit Card

Teenagers who are 18 years or older can obtain a credit card in their own name. Teens under 18 can obtain a supplemental card from parents or other family member. You will be issued a card, but the bill will be included in the primary cardholder's monthly statement.

Parents or guardians can cosign a credit card application. This means that in the event you are unable to make the payments, the cosigner, your parent or guardian, will be held responsible for all unpaid debts.

Finally, you can open a savings or checking account at a local bank and apply for a credit card from the bank. You can be granted a card if you agree to keep a certain amount of money in the account with the understanding that if you do not make your monthly payments the bank will automatically deduct the money from your savings or checking account.

Managing a Credit Card
1. Fees

^ *Credit cards are not free.* Companies charge you to use their cards. There are lots of fees attached to credit cards, and they differ according to the type of credit card. Responsible credit card users are aware of all the fees of all aspects of the account.

^ *Annual fees:* the amount of money the credit card company charges you just to have a card, varies $0-$50 (some cards do not charge an annual fee).

^ *Transaction fees:* the amount charged if you take out a cash advance, is usually higher than your regular interest rate and accrues daily.

^ *Interest rate:* this too varies with cards, some have low introductory rates for a limited time, then the rate increases significantly after the introductory period ends.

^ *Late fees:* all credit cards charge late fees for payments received after the due date, and your interest rate will be increased when you pay late.

2. Pay more than the minimum. The monthly bill states the minimum payment due. Always pay more than the minimum. This will decrease the amount of interest you pay on your balance. Credit card companies make money when you pay only the minimum.

3. Check your monthly statement. Verify your statement each month to make sure you made all the charges that are listed.

4. Keep all receipts. Your receipts from purchases will serve as a second record for your transaction in the event there is an error on your monthly statement.

5. Secure cards. Always keep your card in a safe location and do not lend to anyone, friends or family!

6. Lost or misplaced cards. Report lost or misplaced cards immediately, preferably within 24 hours. Keep a Xerox copy record of the front and back of all your credit cards, and the number to call to report lost or stolen cards in a separate location from your cards.

7. Credit Bureaus. Credit bureaus keep a record of your credit history. It's basically a report card of your credit worthiness, do you pay bills on time, how much you owe, how many times did you pay your bills late, the names of the companies you owe, etc.

Long Term Effects
If you are not responsible with your credit now, it will affect your ability to finance a car loan or home mortgage, get loans to pay for school, and even a career, especially if you are interested in a career in finance.

SAVING AND INVESTING YOUR MONEY

It's an exciting and powerful feeling when you make your own money, but it can be devastating if proper money management skills are not used.

What you do with your money depends on your reason for working. Some teens need to work to help the family, provide for their baby, buy a car, or save for college. Whatever your reason, it is critical that you budget to save a percentage of your income.

Q. Why do I need a budget?
A. Having a budget will help you understand what you can afford. Try not to invest your paycheck in expensive designer brand name clothing and sneakers. Snacks and fast food can also decrease your savings significantly.

Q. Why bother to save?
A. Building wealth begins when you save more than you spend. To afford the things you want now and later, it's imperative to set aside funds that will earn interest and make money for you.

Q. How much should I save?
A. Whenever possible try to set aside at least 50% of your earnings. If that is not possible due to family obligations aim to save between 10-25% each pay period.

Q. Can I invest in the stock market?
A. Yes, you can. Of course, before investing have an in-depth conversation with a trusted adult who can help you figure out your goals and choose a financial advisor to set up your accounts.

Q. Where can I invest my money?
A. There are lots of financial services companies that can help you invest. Again ask your parents, teachers, or other adults to refer you to a creditable investment agency. Take an adult with you and ask lots of questions.

Q. What options do I have if I do not want to invest in the stock market?
A. Open a regular savings account or a CD (Certificate of Deposit) at your local bank or credit union.

CHAPTER TEN

LOOKING OUT FOR NUMBER ONE

. Six Ways to Build Self Esteem

. Six Ways to Cope With Pressure

. Eight Ways to Relieve Stress

SIX WAYS TO BUILD SELF-ESTEEM

1. Do something nice for yourself often.
2. Keep a portfolio with samples of all your successes.
3. Do not beat yourself up when you make mistakes.
4. Find people who believe in you and who will cheer for you always.
5. Set realistic goals.
6. Have a positive attitude.

SIX WAYS TO COPE WITH PRESSURE

1. Remember you are unique.
2. Develop many interests and hobbies to vary the kinds of people you meet.
3. Know that differences are to be celebrated.
4. Believe in yourself.
5. Develop a talent or skill that will help you get to know yourself better.
6. Begin to define and write down your values and moral beliefs.

8 WAYS TO RELIEVE STRESS

1. Set up an action plan.

2. Keep a focus on your goals.

3. Resist negative habits and influences.

4. Develop a spiritual life.

5. Surround yourself with positive people you want to be like.

6. Decrease stressful environments and people in your life.

7. Rethink your priorities in life.

8. Talk to people you trust (friends, parents, school counselor, religious leader), call a teen help line, or join a teen support group.

CHAPTER ELEVEN

EXTRAS TO KNOW

. Five Forbidden Sins on the Job

. The Right Way to Quit a Job

. Be Your Own Boss

FIVE FORBIDDEN SINS ON THE JOB

1. Drug usage of any kind on the job, or coming to work under the influence of any substance, is absolutely unacceptable.

2. Dating someone on the job is not professional. It can jeopardize your job if the relationship does not work out. It can also cause tension among coworkers when the relationship seems to be going well.

3. Stealing money or company property is a criminal offense and you can be prosecuted.

4. Cheating on your time card, whether it's adding 10 minutes or an hour, is still cheating and you can be asked to leave.

5. Weapons of any kind are not allowed on company property.

THE RIGHT WAY TO QUIT A JOB

It happens! Sometimes a job just is not working out, maybe you've outgrown the job, or
you no longer enjoy working with the people,
or a better opportunity has come your way.
Whatever the reason, it's important to end
your relationship with the company the right
way. You might need a reference from
them sometime.

What's the right way to leave?

It is not acceptable or professional to just go in
and say, "I quit," and leave, never to return.
Although you may feel the company deserves
it, that could hurt you later on. The world is a
small place and it pays to end these relationships on a positive note, as you may cross
paths with some of the same people later on
in life.

Keep these rules in mind as you prepare to
leave your job.

1. Write a brief letter of resignation simply
stating that you will be resigning from your

position and give the date you plan to stop working. Don't mention any problems or complaints. You don't really have to give a reason for leaving!

2. Give your employer at least 2 weeks notice before you leave the job.

3. Do not take company property with you when you leave, no matter how small. That is considered stealing.

4. Continue to do a good job until your last day, and if asked, be willing to help the new person.

5. No matter why you are leaving, especially if it is under questionable circumstances, never bad mouth anyone in the company or spread gossip about your situation. It is usually safest not to say anything at all.

BE YOUR OWN BOSS

Sometimes it may not be possible for all teenagers to find a job when they need to and some might want to blaze a new trail. Have no fear, there is a solution. Become your own boss.

Some of the world's most successful million-aires today are people who started their own business. Although you may not become a millionaire just because you own your own business, there is a wonderful sense of accomplishment to know that you are in charge.

Owning your own business however, does not come easy. You still have to work just as hard, if not harder, and often work more hours, too. The biggest difference is that you are the boss and you set all the rules and bear all the responsibilities whether the business does well or it fails.

TEN BUSINESS IDEAS FOR YOU

1. Baby-sitting. Parents will always need a responsible, reliable person to care for their children. If you enjoy children then consider taking a first aid class so you can handle emergencies. Begin to talk to parents in your neighborhood, religious groups, and family friends and let them know you are available.

2. Web Site Designing. Some teenagers are very Internet savvy. If you are and enjoy it, use your skills to build sites for small business owners in your neighborhood. You can go down to your local Small Business Association and ask to put up a sign about your services. The best way is through word of mouth. Build a site for a friend or family member to showcase your skills, ask for a reference, then spread the word.

3. Computer Instructor. Teens who are very adept at working with a computer and enjoy sharing their knowledge can use their skills to teach the ins and outs of computers to senior citizens, other kids, and the many adults who are still not computer literate.

4. Graphic Designing. If you are a great artist and know how to use different art based programs why not offer your services to local religious organizations, camps, and especially small businesses to design their flyers and promotional material.

5. Clowning Around. It may sound funny, but clowns are always wanted at kid's birthday parties and it pays very well. Visit your local costume and joke shops for all the equipment a clown could want then start advertising with friends and neighbors. The word will spread if you are good. You will need a car or a ride.

6. Catering. If your passion is food then consider making sweets, bottled preserves, and other baked goods for all your friends, family, and parents in the neighborhood. Provide samples so they can see how good you are then start taking orders for parties and other special occasions. Be sure to adhere to all food health codes in your area.

7. Yard Care. Regardless of where you live geographically, you will have some of the following: snow to shovel, leaves to rake, lawns to mow, and there will always be home owners who would rather hire students to do that work.

8. Creative Crafts. If you are more of a hands-on type person, consider making jewelry or crafts, knitting or embroidery, or creating attractive accessories.

9. Family Assistant. That's a fancy way to say that you can run errands for people who are unable to do their own errands because their schedules are too busy, or they are shut-in. You can take care of the post office needs, dry cleaning, or even pick up groceries, gifts, or medications.

10. Pet Assistant. Although many people value their pets they are not always able to take care of them. You can offer pet walking services or even be a pet guardian while the owners are on vacation or on business trips.

CONCLUSION

VALUING DIFFERENCES

VALUING DIFFERENCES

To be successful it is important for all employees, teenagers and adults, to be able to work with all people regardless of their ethnicity, religion, race, or personal life choices.

At school, it's easy to avoid the people you do not like because they are probably not in your group, even though they are in your classes. It's probably also easy to exclude them from coming in contact with you.

In the workplace this is not possible. You may be asked to work with someone you do not like or agree with. The important thing to remember is that you are at work get the job done; you are not required to like this person, but you must treat everybody with respect and courtesy.

1. It's not the outward appearance that counts, it's the quality of work.

2. Priority number one is always to get the job done well and on time.

3. Professionalism is not about liking someone, it's learning to respect everyone.

4. When you get to know someone you don't like and find out why they act and think that way, you may be surprised.

5. Right now someone, somewhere does not like you because of how you look, talk, dress, or work. How would you want them to treat you?

Regardless of what you do in life, it's important to know that the things you do now and the decisions you make as a teenager will affect and shape your life negatively or positively. Ultimately you will end up in the work world, and by reading this book you have just received a crash course in how to be an exceptional employee or entrepreneur.

As you work your shifts in the delis, pharmacies, office buildings, retail stores, supermarkets, or parks, know that your number one priority is getting the best possible grades. Those grades, along with the skills you just learned about in this book, and your teenage job experiences will prepare you for that career or business venture you hope to be involved with as an adult.

No one becomes successful by sitting around and daydreaming; it takes hard work, determination, consistency, passion, and the will to press on even when things seem impossible.

People who succeed are people who have a plan and act on it consistently and persistently. Those who do not have a plan are really planning to fail.

Dream big and when you dream know that there are many people waiting for you to take the first step and then they will be there to support you.

Good Luck Always!

HAVE A GREAT LIFE !

Karen Hinds

ABOUT THE AUTHOR

Karen S. Hinds is an international keynote speaker, author, and consultant. She is the founder and president of The Hinds Company, a firm that works with organizations who want to develop employees who are professional and personally effective.

Born and raised in the Caribbean island of St. Vincent, Karen combines her knowledge of Caribbean hospitality, British style, and grace to bring a fresh perspective to improving workplace relationships.

Ms. Hinds has worked extensively with Boston's School-to-Career Movement, coordinating one of its programs.

Karen S. Hinds
P. O. Box 260572
Boston, MA 02126
Tel: (617) 296-5242   Toll free 1-877-902-2775
Fax: (617) 296-6786
Visit us online at: www.Karenspeaks.com
E-mail: Karen@Karenspeaks.com

If you liked this book you will also like

A Teenager's Guide
to the Workplace
Journal

This journal will help teens track their
successes as they learn about the workplace.
It offers practical exercises that will challenge
teens as they make choices on the job and at
school. Topics include goal setting, budget-
ing, how to build a career support network,
how to excel academically, and there is space
for teens to record their thoughts and feelings.

****

YES! YES! YES!

_____ YES! Please add me to your mailing list, so I can learn more about your youth and adult programs.

_____ YES! I want the FREE e-mail subscription to your e-zine "Courtesy Today."

_____ YES! I know of a School, Business, Corporation, or Association that might be interested in on-site training, keynote presentation, or convention breakout. Please call me at my number below.

Name: _____

Phone: _____

Company: _____

Address: _____

_____

E-mail: _____

Phone:_____

For an immediate response, please
call toll free 1-877-902-2775
fax 1-617-296-5242
or e-mail Karen@Karenspeaks.com

Order Form
Books by Karen S. Hinds

Book	Qty	Price
A Teenager's Guide to the Workplace	_____	$15.00
A Teenager's Guide to the Workplace Workbook	_____	$12.00
Get Along, Get Ahead: 101 Courtesies for the New Workplace	_____	$15.00

Shipping and Handling $4.00 1st book, $1.00 each additional book. (MA residents please add 5% sales tax.)
US FUNDS only. Allow 3-5 days for delivery.

My check or money order for $_____is enclosed.

Total $_____

Please charge my:
　　__Visa __MC __American Express

Name:_____

Organization:_____

Address:_____

City:_____ State: _____ Zip:_____

Phone:_____

Fax:_____

E-mail:_____

Card#: _____Exp Date:_____

Signature:_____

Please make check payable and return to: New Books Publishing P.O. Box 260572 Boston, MA 02126

Call credit card order to: 1-877-902-2775

Fax: 617-296-6786. Email: orders@Karenspeaks.com